God is a Loving Father Not an Angry Judge

JAMES A. BORCHERT

GOD IS A LOVING FATHER, NOT AN ANGRY JUDGE

And we have known and believed the love that God hath to us. God is love; and he that dwelleth in love dwelleth in God, and God in him (1 John 4:16).

This book will explore the basics of Christian belief, our Christian life, and our walk. So, where do we start? We start with God. God is the most basic thing. If you get God right and understand Him correctly, if you get the correct view of God, you have solved every problem in the world. There are no other problems. Everything is related to God Himself. If your picture of God is wrong (and there are only two pictures), then everything you decide, everything you do, everything you think, and everything you feel will be affected by that wrong picture (Prov. 23:7). If you get it right, then everything you think, and feel, and want, and do, will be affected by the right picture (Luke 11:34). Only one thing matters: your picture of God. If you forget everything else in this book, if you forget everything else there is, if you get this down, you've got everything down. It may seem very strong to say that just understanding who God is changes everything and affects everything. But it's true. Your view of God affects your faith, your character, and your behavior. It's easy to understand how it affects your faith, but how it affects your character (inner man), and conduct (outer man) may not be so obvious (Ps. 1:2-4; Titus 1:15).

There are two different Greek words for God: *theos* and *theios*. *Theos* is the word used for "God" in the Greek New Testament. When you know God as *theos,* you know Him truly, as He really is, His true self. *Theos* is an intimate and personal knowing of God. When you know Him as *theos*, you are attached to Him and love Him (1 John 4:10, 16). He has revealed Himself through the scriptures as *theos*.

Theios is another Greek word for "God," but by adding the "i," you get a completely different understanding of God. *Theios* is known by every man naturally (Rom. 1:19-20). All men know God as *theios*: God's left hand. Only a handful of people know Him as *theos*: the right hand of God. *Theios* is to know God abstractly. It's not a personal relationship with God; it's to know about Him. (Prov. 1:7; Rom. 2:15). It's an abstract concept, nothing more than a word. It's to acknowledge that there is a God, but you don't know Him personally or intimately. You know Him in the abstract, externally, from the outside. It is similar to asking an acquaintance, "Do you know my wife, Peggy?" And they could answer, "Oh yeah, isn't she the one that...." They may describe her or say something about her and be correct! They may be acquainted with her, but they don't know her. On the other hand, I have a personal relationship with her, a deep understanding of who she is as a person. But I still don't know her as she knows herself. And she doesn't know herself as God knows her. There are different levels of knowing someone.

On God's left hand, we know Him as *theios,* externally. We're acquainted with Him and acknowledge He exists, but it's an abstract concept. If you have a neighbor you have seen but never met, you may recognize him but do not know him personally. It is the same when you know God as *theios*. You don't really know Him; you know about Him. You may know His name, or maybe you know that He's powerful or even merciful. So, you know something about Him, but not very much (Rom. 2:15). You could say that when you know God as *theios,* you don't really know Him at all. Even though you know about Him, you do not truly know Him.

Theos is to know Him intimately, heart-to-heart, how God wants to be known and has revealed Himself to those He chooses to reveal Himself. (Col. 1:26-27; John 17:3). Anybody could know Him as *theos*, even though everyone knows Him as *theios*. An atheist may say, "Well, I don't believe in God. I don't know God," but they do. Even if they say they don't, they do. Everyone knows there is right and wrong, and that God wants you to give Him His due, etc. Everyone knows you shouldn't do wrong, that you're supposed to do right. God is the one that put that awareness in you. Everyone knows God left-handedly (Rom. 2:14-15). Very few know Him right-handedly, including Christians. Most Christians who say *theos* actually mean *theios*. Even though they profess to know Him personally and claim Him as their Savior, it's so abstract to them that you can't tell if they really know Him. You don't see where God is rubbing off on them because they think and act the same as everyone else. Therefore, do they really know Him (1 John 2:15; James 1:22-25; Matt. 7:16-27)?

Is God a loving Father (*theos*) or an angry Judge (*theios*)? Those are the only two pictures of God (Exod. 20:1-22; John 1:17; 15:9). To have an abstract picture of God is to know Him outwardly, externally, not personally or intimately at all. You're not in love with Him (John 5:42; 17:3). You're just simply saying, "Yes, I know Him, I fear Him. I'm trying to do the best I can." But that is not knowing God (Gal. 4:3-7; Phil. 3:8-11). To know God only as a duty is to not know Him at all. The religious idea that "you have to be good" is how most people know Him (Heb. 3:10-12; Rom. 2:28-29). There are two pictures of God: to know Him as every man knows Him and to know Him as He wants to be known and has revealed Himself in the Bible, in the word of God, to His beloved (Col. 1:26-27).

Whether it's in the Old Testament or New Testament, God reveals Himself. That means Mohammed does not know Him, and the Hindus do not know Him. They only know Him left-handedly. They know about God but made up the rest because they don't know enough to understand exactly what He wants or requires. They know He wants something and requires something. They give Him whatever they think, whatever they suppose, whatever they imagine He wants, but that is idolatry. In fact, the Bible calls that kind of worship satanic. It is called devil worship. In the Old Testament, when God revealed Himself to Moses and His people through His word and commands, He said, "When you, to whom I've just revealed Myself, still follow after idols, you are worshiping devils." Why? Because only the devil would put a burden on you and not tell you the heart of God (Exod. 32:19-35; Matt. 23:2-4, 23-26; Gal. 4:3-9; 2 Cor. 11:3). The devil could tell you all about God. He's a terrific theologian! Satan himself is a theologian and can appear as an angel of light, enlightening you about God: "There is a God" (2 Cor. 11:13-15). Even the devil is not arguing over God's existence. He even knows that God made the world. The devil is not claiming that he made it himself – he's saying God made it. But he wants to trip you up in the aspect of worship. He wants you to think God requires you to carry the burden in worship, without receiving any blessing. There's no blessing for you when you follow Satan's pagan worship rituals of God; there's only burden (Acts 15:24; Gal. 2:4-5; 3:1-14).

In human relationships, if you conducted yourself in such a manner, you would be a tyrant. If you only put burdens and pressure on your children or your mate, it would show that you do not have a true picture of God. Your picture of God affects everything in your life. Everything in life that counts and matters is affected by how you see God (Rom. 14:23). There are only two pictures of God. *Theos* is the heart of God, the inside of God, the personal relationship with God where you fall in love with Him (1 John 4:16-19). That can only come by a personal revelation through the preached word of God. *Theios* is the general revelation that all men have by reason and moral conscience. *Theos* and *theios* sound very similar, with just one little "i" difference. But that little "i" is all the difference in the world because, in one case, He's not a loving Father but an angry Judge. Knowing God as *theos*, as your loving Father, will affect all your relationships. You will treat yourself the same way God treats you, and how you treat yourself is how you will treat others (1 John 4:7-12).

Nobody is hard on others before they're first hard on themselves. If you're hard on others, people will have difficulty getting close to and liking you, which would show that you're hard on yourself first. It would also show that you think God is hard on you (Matt. 25:24-30). But if God were forgiving and loving like a father, unconditionally loving you, then you would love yourself and others unconditionally. Your picture of God determines everything in the world (Luke 15:11-24). There is nothing it doesn't affect – absolutely nothing. That's why Jesus came into the world to reveal the true picture of God (John 1:14-18; 17:23-26). Moses gave us a picture, but it was not perfect. I want to say that again: Moses gave you a picture, but he could not give you a perfect picture. Moses told the truth – there was no lie in it. It isn't like Hinduism, Buddhism, Islam, or some other religion. Moses gave the true understanding of God, but it wasn't perfect. In other words, he gave the backside view of God, not the front face of God (Exod. 33:20-23). Only in the face of Jesus Christ do you see the face of God (2 Cor. 4:6). But in the finger of Moses, telling you what to do, you do not see the true face of God (John 1:17; Heb. 8:8-12).

It is so interesting because God presents Himself to Moses and the people of Israel in an alien fashion, not in His true perfection or His full beauty (Exod. 33:23; John 1:18). Even though they know that God is beautiful and perfect and loving, there is now more guilt than ever. They know about God better than the pagans, who only know Him as *theios*, but not much better. Even though they know the truth, the law gives them more guilt than the pagans. The pagans don't know much about God. They just know that there is a God, so they're under a burden to do right and avoid wrong, but that's all they know. They know almost nothing about God. They don't know if He's one God or fifty. The pagans don't have any clarity, so their knowledge is incomplete (Acts 17:30). The Jewish understanding of the Torah is not wrong; it's just not perfect or complete (Heb. 7:19). What it tells you to do, you can't do (Rom. 7:23). Moses can tell you "Be perfect as God is perfect, be ye holy as I am holy, saith the Lord." Well, that's good to know, but you know what? That doesn't add a whole lot to the pagan understanding. It makes it worse because it says you can't do what you think, or feel is right or be sincere about it. You must be exactly like God (Rom. 2:1, 17-25)! That ups the ante. I have to be perfect like God is perfect (Deut. 27:26; James 2:10). What He does, I have to do. I have to do the same thing that He does. Well, I'm not perfect! If you think about it for a moment, you'll realize that you're not perfect; you're not

Jesus. When Jesus was hit in the face, He turned the other cheek. You're not like that; we are not perfect. Moses is telling me something, but he's not helping me. Jesus tells me everything; He forgives me when I fail and then helps me to succeed (Titus 3:4-5). That's different than Moses. The Law came through Moses, but grace and truth came through Jesus Christ (John 1:17).

Do you see the difference? Jesus Christ is showing you the *theos* picture of God. He's not revealing *about* God; He's revealing Him in truth. They told Jesus, "Show us the Father, and we'll be satisfied." He said, "If you've seen Me, you have seen the Father" (John 14:9). Jesus is presenting the true picture of God; there's nothing more important in the world than having the true picture of God (John 3:16-17; 15:9; 16:27).

Now, is God an angry Judge, *theios*, or is He a loving Father, *theos*? Though most Christians believe in Jesus, in the Father, and in the Holy Spirit, they actually live in practical ways, as though they were pagan. Even though they know about Jesus, and they know about the Father, they are not in love with Him. They are legalistic (Gal. 3:1-3; 4:7-9). They're working as though God were an angry Judge. They put pressure on themselves, "I'm not a very good Christian." That is not the confession of someone who's in love; that is evidence of someone who is under pressure (Gal. 1:6; 5:1-6; Col. 2:16-23). "I don't do it very well... I didn't get up this morning..." Do you see the guilt? You can hear the condemnation and the pressure that person carries, and it will affect every relationship they're in.

If you believe that God is an angry Judge, waiting to catch you and evaluating your performance, it will affect your view of yourself and your attitude toward others (1 John 4:7-8). You'll be a performer, and you will force others around you to be performers as well (Rom. 2:17-29; 1 Tim. 1:7). Even if we don't perform very well, we still have high expectations of others and will criticize them when they fail to perform according to our standards (Rom. 2:1). But when we misbehave, we'll blame God. Remember what Adam said? "The woman you gave me – yes, I mis-performed but not too much. I mean, she's the one that did it, really. She was the first one, God! And You're the one that gave her to me, too! I just wanted to point that out..." (Gen. 3:12). That's how we all are in the flesh; it's our nature. If you don't know God as a living God, as a loving Father, you will treat Him as an angry Judge (Isa. 29:13; Matt. 25:24-30; Rom. 2:3-4). And Adam knew, "The day you eat of it, you will die." Whoa! He did not want to say he ate of it, "I know I did eat of it, but she made me eat of it, and You're the one who gave her to me." Immediately he tried to wiggle out of it with a lot of talk. The Adam and Eve story is very interesting. Adam didn't want to feel guilty because he knew he would die if he was. He knows, "Wait, I've just got to say whatever I've got to say – I'll lie if I have to because I don't want to say I was guilty." And so, God asked him, "Well, are you naked?" "Um,

5

kind of ... kind of ... yeah." Adam didn't want to say that, yet you saw how God treated him. He came to Adam and said, "Adam, have you sinned? Did you eat of the tree I told you not to eat of?" That's a law; that would be like *theios*. "Are you imperfect? Did you do wrong? Did you sin?" Adam said, "Well, kind of... not really." But the way he said it was, "The woman You gave me... You gave her to me, and it was the woman's fault. She did that to me, and then I ate, but I wouldn't say it was my fault." Adam tried to get out of it, and God accepted that! He didn't say anything to him (Gen. 3:6-24).

If God were just a lawgiver, an angry Judge, He would have immediately condemned Adam, grabbed him by the scruff of the neck, and said, "You lied to me! I saw you." But remember how God came into the Garden and said, "Adam! Where are you?" He did that as though He didn't know anything. You see, He's alien; He's not being His real self because God knows exactly where Adam is. God knows where Adam is, yet He says, "Adam, where are you?" Isn't that interesting? Why doesn't God say, "Adam, I know exactly where you are because I'm God. I know you're right behind that tree right now with fig leaves sewn on you." And Adam is over there hiding behind the tree, telling Eve, "Get down! Get down! God is looking over in our direction right now." Adam is guilty, but he doesn't want to admit that because if he does, he knows he will be condemned, and then he'll have to be killed. Because he doesn't know who God is, he lies to Him! What if he knew that God loved him unconditionally? If he knew that God was a loving Father, he would come to Him and say, "Father, I've sinned against heaven and You. Forgive me" (Ps. 51:4). Remember the prodigal son? That story showed that he knew the father was a loving father and that he even treated his servants well.

But Adam lies, and so God asks Eve, "Eve, what have you done? You didn't eat of that tree, did you? Did you eat of it and then give it to your husband?" "No, not exactly. I mean, no! I mean the Devil, the snake did that." God also accepts Eve's excuse. But you see, God is not revealing Himself exactly. God knows that she's also lying. And "the day you eat of it" – if God is a law God, He should've killed her on the spot. "Alright, Eve, you just lied." Remember those two people in the New Testament that lied and dropped dead right on the spot? If God is a law God, he should've killed them right on the spot! A lot of people have problems with this because God looks mean in the Old Testament and is a little nicer in the New Testament. But you're not looking at it accurately at all!

God is not *theios*, an angry Judge; He's *theos*, a loving Father (1 John 3:1)! He's a loving Father talking to His child, Adam, and then to His other child, the bride of Adam. Then He accepts their lies. Why? It wasn't based on law. Based on the law, they were guilty and had to die. And they do die, but God, being a loving Father, arranges it so that, even though the law is there, He figures out a way to substitute Jesus into it. But they aren't paying attention to that because they're just trying to escape the law.

But when God comes to the snake, who is looking around for Mrs. Snake, or someone else, he has no one to blame. God doesn't even talk to him, ask any questions, or have a discussion. He immediately said, "Cursed be thou!" Whoa! He should've said that to Adam and Eve, but He didn't because He knows the snake has a head. Who is the head of the snake? Satan. This serpent has a head, and the head of the serpent is Satan. And what does Satan do? He wants to put a burden on you. But God is not an angry Judge placing a burden on you. The Devil is trying to make it look like God is a lawgiver that wants to put you under the law to condemn you and then kill and destroy you. No! No! No! No! That is *theios*, the backside of God, the law side of God, not His true face (Exod. 33:20-23). You don't know God when you only know Him as a lawgiver (Rom. 7:6; 2 Cor. 3:6-18; Heb. 8:6-13).

God is much more than a lawgiver, a ruler, or a judge. God is much more than that! He is also a Redeemer and the Baptizer with the Holy Ghost and with power (Gal. 3:10-14; Luke 24:49). Wow! That's a different God. In that case, He would also be a Forgiver and a Helper. Moses knows nothing about God's forgiveness and help. He only knows a little because of Aaron, who was all about forgiveness. King David was all about power. The prophet, Moses, was given the ministry of the law to show God's people what he requires: perfection. Moses' ministry points to the priest, Aaron, who tells of God's mercy, and Aaron points to King David, a picture of God's power. But the prophet doesn't have mercy. The prophet just relays God's message: be perfect!

There's no bending; there's no mercy. If you broke the limit, you broke it. If you got out of line, you're out of line. And what's the line? Be perfect! You have to be perfect (Gal. 3:10). When the little child is coloring on the paper, he gets out of the line. It doesn't mean anything to him. You may say to the child, "Stay within the lines." They're trying, but their little hand just won't! They scribble all over the page and the table because they can't control it. Their little hand is not able – they see what you're doing and how you stayed within the lines – but they just can't do it. The only way they could do it is if you held their hand and moved it, then they could do it. Do you see how God wants you to enter the kingdom of God as a little child? Let Him guide you. Let Him lead you. Let Him forgive you for getting out of line, and then let Him help you so you don't get out of the lines. It's a beautiful picture of God (Luke 18:16).

Adam and Eve did not know who God was. They knew about Him, but they were lost the minute they ate of the apple, the minute they sinned. They could have turned to God and said, "God, we're sorry," but they didn't know God would forgive them because He hadn't shown that

7

side of Himself yet (Rom. 16:25-26; Eph. 3:4-5). They only knew God as a lawgiver. They didn't know Him as a loving Father. They knew that "God loves us as long as we don't mess up. But what if we mess up?" Every little child born into the world asks, "What will happen if I mess up?" Or "What will happen if my wife catches me doing this?" "What will happen if my husband sees me doing that?" We don't know because we haven't tested that yet.

In the beginning, the relationship is okay, but pretty soon, if performance becomes the basis of the relationship, then I'm going to mess it up because I'm not capable of being perfect. Jesus was perfect, but He was the only one (John 17:4; Heb. 5:9). Jesus being perfect sets the standard, but I can't live up to the standard. And if God is only a lawgiver, then I'm finished! "Oh Lord, if Thou should mark iniquity, who should stand?" (Ps. 130:3). There's no hope for me. If God is *theios,* I'm finished (Rom. 3:19-20). I have to know Him intimately; I have to know if that's not the true picture of God. But that's only the backside of God. Of course, God is a lawgiver, but is that who He really is? If that's who He really is, I'm finished because I've already messed up (Isa. 64:6). I did wrong. I can't do His law; I won't do it; I didn't do it (Rom. 3:10-12). But that's not a good answer; that's not the Adam and Eve answer. They didn't give that kind of answer because they knew it was the wrong answer. Do you know that when little kids know the wrong answer, they won't say it? Instead, they will try and figure out how to move. When they don't know what to say, little kids are just stunned; they're stumped. But Adam immediately thought of something, "I'll blame the wife!" "Yes, I didn't go to work today, but that's because you didn't wake me up. Didn't I tell you to do that?" "No, you did not." "I think I did." A man will always find an excuse for what he did and blame his wife. Anyone that loves you or cares about you – just blame them. And Eve immediately thought, "Huh! I'm not taking that. Okay, it's the snake. The snake made me do that." But the snake didn't have anyone to blame. Who's he going to point to? So, God immediately cursed him. See how He treated Adam and Eve totally differently than He treated the snake? They were not treated in the same manner; He treated them differently.

God was showing Adam and Eve, whether they knew it or not, His loving-Father side, His true side. When you see God as a lawgiver, it's true, He has a law, but it's for Jesus. It's not for you and me (Rom. 5:19-21; 8:1-4). People do not live well under the law (Rom. 7:8-9). If you put pressure on someone – "Hey, don't wear your hair like that" – that's a law, that's pressure. "Don't talk to me like that." That's a law, that's pressure (1 Cor. 15:56). People don't do well like that because they know they will end up doing it or messing it up somehow. Now you're scared that you'll do it, and even if you don't, you're proud that you didn't but scared that you just might. Especially if they push you too far; that's what happens to relationships. If your relationship is built on performance, it's not a relationship.

If God is only *theios,* then you understand God as a lawgiver, as an angry judge (Rom. 9:30-33). If you know Him as *theos,* you know He never expected you to do the law (Rom. 9:15-16; 11:15-16). Let me repeat that: He never expected you to do the Law. "Apart from Me, you can do nothing" (John 15:5). You are not capable of being perfect (Ps. 51:5; Rom. 3:10). When God made Adam and Eve, when He made mankind, when He made you, He was not surprised that you couldn't be perfect. That doesn't mean you can't be made perfect by Him. But you can't make yourself perfect in your own strength, will, and determination. And even when you are perfect, the reason is not that you suddenly discovered an ability to perform – it's because He gave you something (John 3:27). It's because you had a relationship with Him; He did it (Eph. 2:8-10). He forgave you. First of all, He told you what to do, and you didn't do it because you aren't Jesus. Second of all, He forgave you for not being Jesus and imputed righteousness to you (Rom.4:2-5). He said, "I count you as righteous because you believed in Me." I believed Jesus was good; I believed my older Brother was good; I believed He did it right. I know I didn't do it right, and that pleases God (Hab. 2:4; Luke 18:14). But third of all, He baptized you with His Holy Spirit and made you one with Him, intimate with Him so that you know Him by revelation, not just as Savior, but also as Lord (John 16:13; Luke 24:49). He's not only the one that is the holy Example for me, which condemns me, but He's also a merciful Savior who forgives me and counts me as righteous by imputed righteousness, not actual. Then He actually works it in me through the power of the Holy Spirit! But it's not me (Phil. 2:12-13)! It's the Holy Spirit doing it (Eph. 3:20). "It's no longer I that live but Christ that liveth in me, and the life that I now live, I live by the faith of the Son of God" (Gal. 2:20).

It would be one thing if I said to my wife, "Peg, I love you." That would be me loving her, but that is something you cannot do. You cannot love other people because they're not perfect. Sooner or later, they will do something, they will misbehave, they will miss-perform, and it will break the relationship (Rom. 3:12). That's what people do (Eccles. 7:20). But I could say this to my wife: "I don't love you but Christ in me loves you." This is because my love is conditional; it's not God's love. *Theos* love is always unconditional (John 3:16-17; Rom. 5:6-8). He doesn't love you because you're worthy, He doesn't love you because you are worthwhile, He doesn't love you because you're decent, because you're good, or because you're kind. He loves you because you're *not* decent, *not* kind, *not* good (1 Tim. 1:15). That is called unconditional love (1 John 4:10). *Theios* will not let you get away with that. Buddha will not let you get away with that. Hinduism will not let you get away with that. There has to be a caste system in

9

Hinduism, and there has to be an eight-fold way in Buddhism. There has to be because they are all law-based religions, man-at-his-best (Gal. 4:9; Col. 2:8). They're all putting pressure on you to perform. Only true Christianity, not the one that's practiced, not the one that we know, but true Christianity, where God loves you unconditionally and teaches you to love yourself unconditionally, gives you the freedom to forgive yourself, and therefore, you forgive others when they sin. You don't need to forgive people who don't sin, but those who sin against you. That's why there are very few Christians. We tend only to forgive people who we think deserve it or that will benefit from it. We won't forgive people that don't deserve it. If they are Adolf Hitler, or some other kind of monstrous person, like Charles Manson or Jeffrey Dahmer, we don't want to forgive them. But if you don't forgive them, you don't understand that you are no different than they are (Matt. 7:1-5; Rom. 2:1). "Oh yes, I am," you may think. But you're still talking about performance, then, aren't you? You see, in performance, you can measure yourself against someone else, "Well, I did better… The woman Thou gavest me… The snake did it." I blame someone else, as though I'm better, saying, "I may not be perfect, but I'm better!" (James 4:11-12). But God's standard is perfection. He doesn't accept "better." There is no such thing as "better." There's only perfect. You have to be exactly like Jesus. Listen carefully to His law: "Be perfect as I am perfect: be holy as I am holy" (1 Pet. 1:16). That is the law. And if that's true, my licentious behavior is wrong, but so is my legalism. Everything is wrong. Everything I do, anything I do, all things I do, are wrong because God is good, only God is good, none is good but God, and I'm no good (Rom. 3:10-12; Isa. 64:6). That's the only way. How am I ever going to get good? If I'm not God, because only God is good, and none is good but God, and I'm "none," then how will I ever get good? You can't! You will never have goodness in yourself (Mark 10:18). You'll never have love, joy, peace, patience, kindness, goodness, or gentleness. But you will have Jesus, who *is* love, patience, kindness, goodness, and gentleness (1 Cor. 1:30-31; 1 John 4:17). You yourself will never have it; you can have a relationship, but you cannot have a performance except in the relationship where He does it all (John 15:4-5; Gal. 2:19-20). The Holy Spirit is in you to will. The Holy Spirit is in you to do. The Holy Spirit is doing it (Phil. 2:12-13). He's the one operating it (Phil. 1:6). You are not good, so you can't do good (Luke 18:19)! If you ever did good, you would know it wasn't you; you would know it was God. That's why worship, which our church is looking at this year, is something that comes out of nothing, because you don't have it (Phil. 3:3; Rom. 4:6-7; 2 Cor. 12:9-10). You can't worship. It has to be, "Thank you, Jesus, for doing it all," not for me adding to what You have done or making a nice work called "worship" (Eph. 2:8-10). Worship is the recognition that there is nothing to be done. It has all been done by Jesus, and now, through the Holy Spirit, I'm doing some things, like worship, but it's a work of God! It's wrought in God; it's not me working it (Eph. 1:3-6, 19-20; 3:20-21; Heb. 13:21). I don't love my wife, I don't love you, I don't love anybody. I don't love myself. I don't love! I could have a conditional kind of love, but it's just that: conditional. Even I myself am hard on myself at times, even as a Christian. I'll forget and just say, "What you just did right there, that was awful. You are a terrible person." I went from doing an awful deed to being a terrible person because I was the tree that produced that fruit. And I'll blame myself even though I know the good theology. I'll catch myself every once in a while, saying, "Oh, I hate that. Oh God, I am so lowly." And I'll loathe myself. Everyone does this. It doesn't matter if you just think it or if you say it. Everyone gets to that point; it doesn't matter whether you think it or say it, "I wish I were dead right now; I hate what I just said. Why did I say that? Why did I do that? God, I hate myself." That path took me from doing to hating self (Job 3:3). Relationships are totally based on something, some rock. You can build it on the sand of performance or the Rock of God's unconditional love (Matt. 7:21-27). Is He a loving Father or an angry Judge?

This is the foundation and basis of everything: there are only two pictures of God. Either He is a loving Father, or He's an angry Judge. The whole world knows Him as an angry Judge. Almost no one knows Him as a loving Father, including Christians. They know the words, but they don't know the reality. When you know Him as a loving Father, which is the only way to know Him truly, it will result in you loving yourself. If He loves you while you are yet a sinner, not after you have tried to fix yourself up, and He's perfect and knows exactly how to love perfectly, then you can love yourself. I hate the deed, but I can love myself because He loves me (1 John 4:16-19). He's chosen me as His beloved (2 Thess. 2:13). Then the Holy Spirit starts working on me because I'm in a relationship – the Spirit is a relationship thing (John 14:16-20; 2 Cor. 3:17-18). Jesus dying on the cross is not a relationship. That's something He did that I either believe or don't believe. It's not a relationship until He baptizes me in the Holy Spirit (Luke 24:49). Now I'm in a relationship with Him, and all kinds of good works come out. But I didn't do them; the relationship did them (Eph. 3:16-20). That is, He did them, not I. It's no longer "I," it's a new "I" (Gal. 2:20; 2 Cor. 5:17). That "I" is now a box that contains something; it's a building that has something in it. If I'm a container of God, God comes out of the container (John 15:4-5). But He loves the container first before He comes out and loves other people through the container. Do you see? If I'm a temple, I'm the temple of the Holy Spirit. That means it isn't me loving; it's the One who is in the temple, in the cup, in the vessel, in the box. It's the Holy Spirit, the presence of God, who does that (Col. 1:11, 27). The Holy Spirit is showing me the living, intimate heart of God (John 14:26). He's not

11

showing me a God that created the heavens and the earth, some external guy. He's not showing me Jesus, who died on the Cross. He's showing me the heart of the living God and giving me a personal, intimate, heart-to-heart, Spirit-to-spirit revelation. I am one with Him (John 16:13-15). That's the work of the Spirit (1 John 2:27). He's constantly leading us, guiding us. And to what end? To perform? No! To be in relationship. "Beholding Him, we are changed" (2 Cor. 3:17-18). The change is the result of the beholding. The beholding is what I'm doing (Rom. 6:11-12; 12:2). He's putting Jesus before me. But which Jesus? The Jesus as a lawgiver? No! No! No! That's not Jesus. That's Moses (John 1:17). That's God in His Moses-picture. But Moses only saw the backside of God, not the face (Exod. 33:20-23). Remember, Moses was hidden in the cleft of a rock. God used His hand to cover his face from His servant, so that all Moses could see was the backside of God. He saw the backside of the glory of God: "Thou shalt not!" That's negative, the backside. "Thou shalt not have other gods.... Thou shalt not kill. Thou shalt not commit adultery." I see the "not" side of God, but I don't see the face of God until I see Jesus (John 1:14; 2 Cor. 4:6). "Show us the Father, and we'll be satisfied..." "If you've seen Me, you've seen the Father" (John 14:9-10). Do you see that?

If you're in an intimate relationship with Jesus, you're not under pressure (Matt. 11:28-30). I can tell when someone is a Christian, and it's not because they come to church or profess Jesus and say, "I believe in Jesus." That doesn't show me anything at all. When I look at the fruit, I can tell "that person is at rest... that person is not working... that person is not a performer, they're a lover" (Heb. 4:10). Lovers always make it. Performers will always get caught short (Matt. 25:1-12; 4:1). Sooner or later, a performer will fall apart because we just can't perform (Isa. 28:12-13; Matt. 7:24-27). It has to be Him! It's a relationship (John 15:4-6). You have to be in an intimate, loving relationship with Him, which he initiates. You have to know that He loves you unconditionally – no conditions, without you doing anything (John 15:9; 17:23-26). You don't have to do anything to please Him (John 6:28-29). You've done a lot of things that were not right, not perfect, but don't think on them. Think on the one thing Jesus did for you that was right (Luke 10:39-42). Focus on that instead. That will release you to love yourself and say, "You know what? I'm not worthy, but Jesus loves me. I'm going to believe it; I'm going to let that renew me. If I strive right now to try and clean up my act, I'll probably mess up again." It takes all the pressure away from you (1 John 4:16-19; Rom. 5:17; 8:1-6).

On the sixth day, He created man, and on the seventh day, He didn't say, "Man, let's go to work!" He said, "Enter into My rest forever" (Heb. 4:1-12). Remember? But man, however, couldn't live with that. He started eating the apple. He started performing. And God was saying, "Don't try to get knowledge of Me, of good and evil. Don't try to get that apart from Me. Don't eat of that tree. You're not going to get anywhere that way" (Gen. 2:17). If you try to be a good person, you'll never make it. You can't do it (Rom. 7:18). The Tree of Life is the one you need to eat (John 6:51-53). Jesus said, "I came that you might have life" (John 10:10). He gave you fruit out of another tree (Rom. 14:17). Don't eat of the other tree, where you're trying to be good apart from God. You'll just be evil (1 Cor. 15:56). It's not a tree of the knowledge of good and evil; it's a tree of knowing about good and evil, "I know there's good, and I know there's evil, but I don't know how to do it. I can't perfect myself because 'good' actually means perfect; it's not just "do the best I can," (Matt. 5:48). If I thought God said, "Please Jim, just do the best you can." Well, then, that is something I could do. I could justify anything I've done and say, "Well, that's the best I could do under the circumstances." "But you just hit your sister!" "I know, but that's because she just kicked me, and that's the best I could do." "No, you know I told you not to do that." Parents want perfection. They want you to do what they say, "Come to the table... Come right now. Make your bed. Take that shirt off and put this one on." Parents want the child to behave. But what happens when they don't?

We were with five grandchildren this weekend, and guess what? With five grandchildren, one of them is bound to mess up. When they do, yes, you can spank them, but that does not stop their behavior or make them behave; it makes them act like hypocrites. They still want to punch their sister and, given an opportunity, when you're not looking, or you're not right there clamping down on them, they'll do it because they were just hypocrites. When they pretended they got along, they were just pretending. Because as soon as that other person does anything to irritate them, they will smack them, hit them, or run from them. They're going to get into trouble. All the law can do is make you a hypocrite. The highest you can ever get under the law is hypocrisy (Isa. 29:13). It's not genuine, perfect love. What God wants is, "Be ye perfect as I am perfect, be holy as I am holy" (1 Pet. 1:16). Don't be a legalistic, law-keeping, outward kind of holy (Luke 11:39-40). But the truth is, I can't even do that. Legalists can't even legalistically be legalistic! Even hypocrisy is tough because the law does not say, "Love the Lord thy God with half thy heart." You're actually supposed to love Him with all your heart and all your soul and all your strength (Deut. 6:5). It's too much! But God says, "No, I created you: heart, soul, and strength. I want all of you. I want all your worship. I want you to be exactly like I am. I want your heart to be like Me. I want your soul to be like Me. I want your body to be like Me. I want everything you say, do, and think to be like Me. I want all of you" (1 Thess. 5:23-24). "Well, I can't! I can't! I won't! I didn't. So now what?" If God is an angry Judge, you're in trouble. But what if He's a loving Father? And I will tell you right now: God is a loving Father (John 17:23, 26; 1 John 4:16-19). If you have that view and you meditate and chew on that, then your whole life will be blessed. Do not meditate on the law and chew on that because the law will only make you either guilty or proud. It will make you a hypocrite or licentious. That's all the law can do! Because the law is not something you can do (Rom. 7:18-24). You cannot "do."

Nobody can do the Law from the heart. Not perfectly! The letter of the law kills, but the Spirit of the law… What is the Spirit of the Law (2 Cor. 3:6, 17)? Ahhh! That's where you have to go beyond the law (Rom. 2:29; 7:6). You have to read between the lines of the law and get past the negative backside of God. You have to see the face of Jesus in the Law because He is the end of the Law (Rom. 10:4; Heb. 7:18-19). Jesus is the perfection of the law (Rom. 8:3-4; Heb. 10:7-10).

If I want to be perfect, I have to go through Jesus; I have to have Him as my foundation. Don't look at God as a lawgiver because you won't get in that way (Col. 2:20-23; Gal. 2:19-20). I have to see God as the merciful One, and I have to come to Him as a sinner (Rom. 4:5-6). Then He will give me the Holy Spirit as proof that I believed He was a forgiver (Eph. 1:13). And when I have the power of the Holy Spirit, I can do all things. "I can do all things through Him that strengthens me" (Phil. 4:13). But I can do nothing apart from Him (John 15:5). Obviously, "Him" is the issue. Relationship is the issue, not performance (John 15:4-5; Col. 1:23; 2:6-8). I can do nothing – that's performance. I can do all things – that's performance – but the key is that I can do nothing apart from Him and everything through Him. The key is the relationship. Jesus is the key, showing you the true face of God. He loves you unconditionally. Can you start to see that now?

If you learn this one lesson, you will know everything in the world. Don't learn it with your head; learn it in your heart, deep. Get it from *theos,* the living God, not *theios*. Right Hand: *theos*. Left Hand: *theios*. You could read all through the Bible, and you'll see that God always distinguishes His right hand from His left hand. The right hand is always to see God as He really is. That's where His power is; that's where His glory is, where his mercy is, where His strength is (Ps. 16:11; 44:3; Isa. 41:10). The left hand is always the Law (Gal. 3:11-12; Matt. 25:41).

If the Law is understood according to the letter of it, it refers to God's left hand. But if the law is understood according to the spirit of it, then it is fulfilled under the Gospel of Christ, but you do not do it. Rather it is fulfilled by Christ for me as a forgiven, born-again "me," a filled-with-the-Spirit "me," a baptized-in-the-Holy-Ghost "me." Once the Gospel fulfills the law, it giveth life (Rom. 7:4; 8:1-4; 2 Cor. 3:6, 17-18). Then you are perfect (Heb. 10:14).

The secret to our church is really not very deep. But that doesn't mean it's being lived. That doesn't mean it's being understood. It's not a matter of understanding; it's a matter of hanging on to the fact that you're in a loving relationship. If you know God is a loving Father, you're going to love yourself, and you're going to love your neighbor as you love yourself (1 John 4:12). To the same extent that I love myself, I'll love my neighbor. To the extent I hate myself, I'll hate my neighbor. And to that extent, it shows that I don't know who God is. It's proof positive that you don't truly know who God is. If you're hard on yourself, you don't know God. If you're hard on others, you don't know God. People can feel that fruit coming out from you, "You're tough to be around... You're hard to be around... You're full of pressure... You're always putting pressure on me..." Marriages fall apart for exactly this reason: someone is putting up a fence, "Don't cross that line right there." Except, I will. I don't care what line you come up with or what fence you make. No matter how broad, or narrow, it will be crossed sooner or later. In an intimate marriage relationship, it's impossible to avoid all those fences. Sooner or later, they will be crossed.

"Boy, one thing I can't stand is a liar." Well, guess what? Sooner or later, that other person is going to lie. That statement also indicates your own capacity for lying, and you don't even know it! You're so blinded by the thought that lying is unforgivable, that you think you never lie (Rom. 2:1-4). "My father lied, and I couldn't stand it, so I don't want to marry anyone who's a liar." But are you a liar? Whatever your hang-up is, that's likely the person you will marry. You better work this out with Jesus and get that relationship down first: God is a loving Father. You must first understand that He will never turn against you, that He's not waiting for you to perform, and in fact, He doesn't even want you to perform (Rom. 8:31; Gal. 4:7; 5:1). He loved you while you were yet a sinner (Rom. 5:8). He never told you to perform. You might say, "Yes, he did, Pastor." No, He didn't (Col. 2:20; 3:3). You're looking at the wrong side of God; you're seeing Him through the law (2 Cor. 3:13-18). "Well, He said it." Yes, I know, but He didn't mean for you to do it; He meant for you to say, "I can't" (Rom. 5:20; 7:23-24). He said, "Be perfect," so you'd say, "I can't." He didn't say it so you would do it. He said it so you would be exposed as a non-doer, and you would say, "I can't." But you won't say that if you don't know His true face. Everyone who knows God as a law person will do the same thing Adam did and say, "I didn't do it... I mean, I did it, but it wasn't my fault." They will all make some kind of similar silly statement. Why? Because they don't know His face (Rom. 2:4; 2 Cor. 4:3-6). If you knew that your Father in heaven loved you unconditionally, it would totally alter your life and the lives of everyone around you. If you could see the true God, see Him face-to-face, see Him through the face of Jesus, everything in the world would be different. In this world, you will not see Him face-to-face. No one can see God and live. You can see Him through the Gospel, but not through the law (John 1:14; 2 Cor. 3:17-18).

15

God has three different faces: 1) the face of holiness, 2) the face of mercy, and 3) the face of power. Mercy and power come through Jesus Christ. The law comes through Moses, but truth and mercy come from Jesus (John 1:17). The baptism of the Holy Spirit is the third face, the last one. You will only see the merciful Savior, number two, if you fail number one (the Law). I don't need mercy unless I have messed up (Gal. 3:24). That's why he makes the law so strong. He says, "Be perfect!" If He had just said, "Be the best you can," then He'd say, "Jim, were you the best you could?" "Yes, sir!" "But you just hit her!" "Well, I know, but that's because she hit me first." You see, that was the best I could do. "I wasn't going to hit her, except she hit me. And as soon as I hit her and knocked her down, I didn't keep hitting her." I can justify that. Even though I did wrong and admit I did wrong, I wasn't perfect because the law only required that I do my best. But God gives the perfect law and says, "Stop all that. I want you to be perfect, exactly as I am." "Oh, that's what perfect means? Be exactly like you? Christ-like? Just like Christ? Uhhh… I can't do that." You would then quickly leave and abandon the law side of God, the performance side, and go over to the Gospel side (Gal. 2:19-20). That is the purpose of the law: to drive you to the Gospel (Rom. 7:24-25). The purpose of the law was never to get you to do it (Rom. 3:19-20; 5:20). Only Jesus does it. The law was written for Jesus, not you (Matt. 5:17-18; Rom. 5:18-19). He takes the burden and gives you the blessing (Gal. 3:13-14; 2 Cor. 5:21). Why? Because His true face is that of a loving Father, not an angry Judge (Eph. 2:4-10). An angry Judge wants you to perform and will cut you off when you don't, but a loving Father will love you no matter what, forgive you, and then help you to do it (Rom. 5:8-10; 8:31-37). Whew! That's a totally different picture of God. There's nothing wrong with the first face (the Law); it just doesn't belong to you because you cannot be perfect; you're not God. Only God is good (Mark 10:18). He wants a relationship. He's trying to get a relationship with you; He doesn't want your performance (Gal. 2:19-20). He doesn't want a servant who performs; He wants a son who loves (Gal. 4:4-7). If I told Peggy, my wife, "Peggy, I don't care what you do or don't do. I don't care how you perform; I don't care if you cook for me, or if you spit at me, or if you're kind to me, or kind one second and hateful the next second, and then kind the next second and hateful the next. I don't care how you are; I love you unconditionally. I'll never leave you nor forsake you, don't worry about it" (Eph. 5:25). Wow! That gives her a lot of freedom because she doesn't have to wonder, "What if I do this? Then he'll reject me. What if I say this? Then he'll reject me." Now she won't have to think about it or wonder anymore. I've solved it by showing her unconditional love: "Peg, there's nothing you can do to make me happy or unhappy because I'm not into performance. I'm into relationship. I want to be married to you" (Hosea 2:19-20). I want her to be calm: I'm not looking for a better wife. I do not love her so she will love me. I just love her because Jesus said, "Jim, that's who you are!" I didn't know that! Before He told me who I am, I wouldn't have been kind. I'm mean and nasty in the flesh, and it'll come right out of me. If you catch me off guard a little bit, you'll see my old self come right out. That snake is not in the garden; it's in me (1 Tim. 1:15). The snake will just come right out and bite you. It can come out really fast, even though I'm a pastor and perform so nicely. If you catch me off guard, you'll see that other side of me that Peggy sees at home.

God sets me free from all of that. Do you know what he says? "Jim, whoa! What are you doing?" "I'm just snaking." "Well, stop that." "I can't! She made me do it. The woman You gave me made me do it, you see!" When I married her, I thought she would just be happy with me. I thought she would think it was great to be married to me! I just could not imagine the problem. I'm not an alcoholic. Man! She should be really grateful! I don't commit adultery... She should be doubly grateful! So many men do! I'm not an alcoholic, and I'm not an adulterer. I'm not even thinking about it. That's wonderful! But that doesn't have anything to do with love. I just didn't misbehave in those two areas. There are a lot of other areas, though, where I'm very selfish. If she asked something like, "Jim, do you love me?" "Hmmm. What does that mean? That's a tricky word, 'Do you love me?'" You see, I don't know how to answer. If she said, "Christ in you loves me," it could be true. I have no problem there. But she's asking, "Do *you* love me?" "You mean, like, could you depend upon me from now on? Is that what you're asking? Are you looking for me to be your God? Because if that's what you're saying, then no. Let's get that over with right away. Don't even go there. If I take you out tonight, and it looks like love, and I say really nice things for a while, then you'd probably expect me to keep going. You would want it for an hour, maybe two, but I just can't last that long." I'm sure I'll be boring or uninterested, or I won't care in a few minutes, or I'll be watching TV or doing something else. Performance-based relationships are not relationships of love for real people.

It took us about 20 years, maybe 25, to get rid of that. Let's not judge each other according to the flesh. "If any man be in Christ, he's a new creation, the old has passed away, the new has come" (2 Cor. 5:17). We once regarded Christ from a human point of view, but let's not regard him thus any longer. Similarly, don't look at people from a human point of view (2 Cor. 5:16). It won't come out right. You will end up putting pressure on them, "Peg, the reason I was mad tonight is because of what you did." You see, I'll put blame and pressure on her. "You said thus and so at the supper table." "Yes, but four years ago, you did this, and I haven't forgotten that either." We can put pressure and law on people, but is that who God is, an angry Judge? Or is He a loving Father? People don't do well under anger.

Are you aware of that? You don't do well when someone is angry at you for misbehaving, either. Are you aware of that? Little kids do not thrive under anger. They feel awful. Little kids are sensitive to it, "Do you hate me now? Don't you love me?" I don't care what you say to them after that; they felt the pressure of it. They know that, somehow, they're guilty. They pick up on that. Because we're not perfect. You can say, "Sweetheart, this has nothing to do with you," but it doesn't help. I don't care what you say to them; it doesn't help. They'll even agree with you, "Okay, I know, Mom." They're just saying that, but it's not what they're really thinking on the inside. They still feel the pressure: "I didn't do right, did I?" If there's a parental problem, the children take it in, "I did that. I know I caused that. If I had been a better boy, this wouldn't have happened... If I had been a better girl... I know you told me to make my bed the other day, and I didn't do it. I probably caused that." That's just the way children think! Even us, as adults, think somehow, we caused it. We are to blame for it; it's our fault. Other people will blame us too. "Yes, it is – it's your fault. If you hadn't done that, this wouldn't have happened." You're under the law! Everything in the world is law because that's the only picture they have of God! We're not looking to God to save America. We're looking to our satellites, and we're looking to ourselves, we're looking to some performance, "If we'll all pull together as a country...." First of all, it'll never happen. But second of all, it's a fruitless answer. If we'll all pull together? What? Are you living in Utopia? This country is divided right down the middle.

Do you think some magic person will come along, some wonderful guru, some Obama or John McCain or Huckaby or Hillary? None of them can do it. Those are the only options we have, but none of them can pull us together. None of them! Why? Because we're not going to be pulled together. We're pulled apart. We have different views of everything, totally and completely different. We are not one nation; we are not united. We have all kinds of people in this country that don't like us, and the rest of us don't like each other either. We won't have unity. We don't get along as families. We don't even get along with ourselves. That kind of naïve thinking shows one thing and one thing only: you still think of God as a pressure guy, as someone who is an angry Judge rather than a loving Father.

Everything in life depends on our picture of God. In other words, what He looks like. Knowing exactly who God is will determine everything else in our lives (Heb. 10:38). "The just shall live by faith." That's face number two that we talked about earlier. "If any man draws back, my soul shall have no pleasure in him." But we are not of them that draw back unto perdition, but of them that believe to the saving of the soul (Heb. 10:39). There's no law here; it's faith. You have to have faith; otherwise, it won't work. The next Scripture: "God has not cast away his people whom he foreknew. Behold, therefore, the goodness and severity of God," – so God is good, and God is severe – "on them which fell: severity" – that's one picture of God – "but toward you, goodness, if you continue in His goodness," (Rom. 11:22). "Oh no!" you might think, "See, I'm under the Law." No, it doesn't mean that! The goodness that He's talking about is not under the Law. The goodness He's talking about is under the Gospel (Rom. 2:4). Why? Because He says to continue in that. Not continue in the law, not continue performance but continue in knowing that He wants a relationship with you. Why? Because that's the only thing that will produce that goodness. You see, you could read that and get condemned. But you could also read that and get set free. I'm telling you how to read it. If you read it as "You must continue in His goodness, otherwise you'll be cut off," it sounds like you're under the law. No! Being cut off is just a fact. If you don't go by faith, you'll go by works (Rom. 11:6). If you don't see God as a loving Father, you'll drop back into an angry Judge. That's what it's saying. But I know how everyone reads it – and God knows that too. He knows He will catch everyone on that because you want to look at God as an angry Judge. You're free to. But if you want to look at God as a loving Father, you're also free to (Titus 1:15). He's telling you something: there's nothing but love in God (1 John 4:16). As you go through this book, you're going to begin to see how loving God is, how everything about God is love (Ps. 36:7-9).

There are only two pictures of God: either He is our loving Father, or he is an angry Judge (Matt. 25:14-30). All of our problems in life result from a basic misunderstanding or confusion about who God is. It's absolutely vital to know the truth. Don't be confused; be clear about this: God is a loving Father. Simple! He is not an angry Judge (1 John 4:10, 16-19).

The truth is that God is our loving Father. He is not an angry Judge. The Scripture says, "For God so loved the Church..." No! It says, "For God so loved the world." If He only loved the Church, He would be an angry Judge with a law. Only Church people would qualify, and non-church people wouldn't. But He so loved the world! Why? Because He's an unconditionally loving God. He wants everyone to be saved, even "bad" people. Why? Because that's all there is (bad people) (John 3:16-17)! That's all there is. He wants bad people to be saved because I'm one of the bad people. God is not choosing people; He's not a respecter of persons. He's not into performance. He's into relationship (John 15:4-5; John 17:19-26).

The Scripture says, "For God so loved the world that He gave His only begotten Son, that whosoever should believe in Him should not perish but have eternal life" (John 3:16). That means everlasting. The Scripture says, "God desires not the death of any sinner" (Ezekiel 33:11). What about Adolf Hitler? Didn't God want his death? What about Charles Manson? What about Pharaoh? Didn't God want Pharaoh to die? He gave him ten chances! He didn't want Pharaoh to die; He wanted Pharaoh to repent. He knew he would not, but that doesn't mean He didn't give him ten chances. If you want to kill him, just give him one chance, or just kill him. But He wanted to give him many chances. He kept going from flies to mosquitoes to gnats and so on to try to get him to soften. God said, "Hey! Do I have to use a cannon, or what? Okay, I'll take your firstborn." But Pharoah knew, "No, you won't because my firstborn is the son of God." Well, he found out who was God and who was not. God did that, not because He hated him, but because He loved him. You may say, "Well, God hardened Pharaoh's heart." I know, but if you read the Bible, it will also say, "Pharaoh hardened his heart," and God went along with it. But my point is this: God is still a loving Father, even to Pharaoh. Did He want Pharaoh to die? This Scripture says He didn't (1 Tim. 2:4; 2 Pet. 3:9). You'll have to decide whether you want to read where it says, "God hated Esau," or whether you're going to believe that God loves all men. Do you believe God loved the world (John 3:16-17; Rom. 10:13)? He loved Esau! He loved Pharaoh! He loved Hitler! He loved everyone! You are wrong! "Yeah, but it says that!" I don't care what it says. You're reading it wrong. You're reading it under the Law (John 5:39-40, 45-47; 2 Cor. 3:14-18; 4:4). Don't read it according to the letter that killeth, but according to the Spirit that giveth life (John 14:17, 26; 1 Cor. 2:9-10; Eph. 1:18-19). We are so determined to make God out to be ugly rather than see the truth. You are so used to the Law that you're not used to mercy yet (Acts 26:18).

What if Pharoah had humbled himself? Do you know who did just that? King David. King David broke the law. He took the wife of his best friend, Uriah, and slept with her. Then he had Uriah killed to cover his sin. That is evil. Then he lied about it! He broke three commandments. He broke every commandment in the book, yet God calls him a man after His own heart (Acts 13:22). Why is that? Because even though David did that (and he was stubborn!), when God finally pointed it out to him, David said this: "God, against Thee and Thee only have I sinned" (Ps. 51:4). God could've said, "You sinned against Uriah. You sinned against Bathsheba. You sinned against the people of Israel. You sinned against yourself. You sinned against a lot of people." But David said, "No, I've sinned against You. I know what my sin is, and it's deep. I did not trust You. And yet, in my heart, I'm a believer." Do you see the difference? When he humbled himself, what did God do? He answered his prayer: "Create in me a new heart, O God" (Ps. 51:10). He answered his prayer because King David was not under the law; he was under the Gospel (Ps. 51:12).

The Scripture also says, "His thoughts towards us are always thoughts of peace" (Jer. 29:11). Paul writes in Romans 5:8, "God commends His love toward us in that, while we were yet sinners, Christ died for us." Who is He loving? Non-sinners or sinners? John writes in 1

John 3:1, "Behold what manner of love the Father has bestowed on us that we should be called the sons of God." What is God after? Performance or sonship? Does He want you to be a slave, a servant? Or does He want you to be a son (Gal. 4:5-7)? He's not after performance; He's after relationship. Make the tree good, and the fruit will be good (Matt. 12:33).

John declares in 1 John 4:8-9, "For God is love. In this was manifested the love of God toward us because He sent his only begotten Son into the world that we might believe through Him or live through Him." Once we are convinced that God is love and that He loves us with a perfect love, unconditionally, then we will return love to Him and show love to others. The Bible says, "We love because He first loved us" (1 John 4:19). Your love is totally dependent on His loving you first. You can't "perform" love because you don't have any unless you have God in you. You have to have God in you to love because God is love. You can't love unless He first loved you. His love is not to enable you to keep the law; His love is that He keeps the law for you and in you and through you (Isa. 26:12; Phil. 2:13). He does it all. To God be the glory (1 Cor. 1:30-31)!

This is very powerful. The reason that Peggy and I have a good marriage is not because we're performing; it's because we believe God loves us. I believe God loves Peggy just the way she is. I don't believe I have a right to criticize her, no matter what she does. I don't believe I have a right to regard her from a human point of view because it's not performance we're after but a relationship. I love my wife just the way she is, not fixed-up. I don't want her to improve. I don't want her to be nice to me. I want her to be whatever she wants to be because God loves me that way, and I'm instructing her in the same way. I don't love her because she loves me back. I'm not going to love her because of anything in her. I don't care if she ever loves me back. I don't care! I'm not interested in that. When she does, thank God. But I don't thank her, I thank God. I don't thank her because that would put pressure on her, "Well, Peg, now there, I give you an "A" on that one. You did good right there." I don't do that to my wife. I won't do it. "Now, Peggy, I liked that part right there." That would be putting pressure on her. Do you understand what I'm saying? She's easily given to pressure because she was raised legalistically and always did the right thing. She has a quick tendency to slip into guilt. I don't have that. It's really hard to make me feel guilty about anything. In fact, it's probably impossible. I just don't feel guilty. When the Holy Spirit is inside of you, He changes you. I don't have my eye on Jim performing. I have my eye on Jesus, who already did the performing. Why? Because He did that out of His love for me. And I know it was only relationship; it had nothing to do with performance. He shouldn't have performed toward me because I don't deserve anything. I deserve death! I ate of the Tree. But He didn't curse me; He cursed the snake (Gen. 3:15). The Father that loves me did not want me to die, even though I deserve to die, so He sent Jesus to die in my place. He died my death for me so that I could live and not die. Thank you, God, for cursing the snake and not me! Thank you, God, for sending Jesus to die in my place (John 3:16).

In the Old Testament, God is doing His alien work (Col. 1:26; Eph. 3:9). An alien is a foreigner. God Himself is a stranger. What does that mean? He shows himself as face number one: a holy lawgiver (Exod. 33:22-23; Gal. 3:23-26). But that's not who God truly is. That law is for Jesus (John 4:34; 19:30; Rom. 5:19; Heb. 10:9-10). Then why did He show it to me? To drive me to Jesus, who kept it for me, so that I'll say, "You know what God? I can't keep that law, I'm not perfect (Rom.3:19; Gal. 3:24). But I'm going to believe in Jesus who is," (Rom. 3:21-24). Now that's exactly what God wanted! Do you see our relationship now (Gal. 2:19-20)? And how I'm so grateful for that relationship now? I didn't perform. I just thanked Him for performing (Rom. 4:5-6). There's nothing more to do. Jesus did it all (Heb. 4:10-11; 2 Cor. 5:17, 21)! I'm thanking Him and worshiping Him, not as a work, but as thanksgiving that I don't have to do any work because He did it all (Col. 2:6-7). That is pure worship. Worship is where He did it all, and I'm only thanking Him for doing it all (Rom. 5:11). I'm not worshiping so He'll like me because I'm worshiping Him. No, I'm thanking Him because He likes me even before I worship Him. He just likes me. That's why I'm thanking Him (Eph. 1:3-6). I'm always thankful to people that like me. When people like me, I know they're either crazy or don't know me well because if you really knew me, you wouldn't like me. But God says, "No, Jim, I do like you, and I know everything about you" (Rom. 5:8; 1 John 4:10). Wow! That's why I thank him (Rom. 4:4-10). I say, "Jesus, I can't believe you like me. I don't even like me." When other people don't like me, I admire them because they're so smart. Do you see that? It's a free gift (Rom. 5:17).

In the Old Testament, God is doing His alien work. He is shows Himself as a lawgiver when He's actually a loving Father. He presents Himself as an angry Judge, but only to cause us to repent and say, "I can't keep the law!" (Rom. 3:19-20). Moses only showed us the backside of God, God as a lawgiver, to expose our sinfulness so that we would turn to Him in faith (Rom. 7:7-10, 24-25). In other words, He shuts one door to open the other (Gal. 2:19-20; 3:22-26). When I see how perfect God is, I know that I'm not like that. I can't do it. I can't perform. I'm not perfect. I don't even think I'm good. In fact, I know I'm not good at all (Rom. 7:24). "If what You said is true, I'm not good at all." The Old Testament is all about repentance, which means He only showed us His Holiness to drive us to His righteousness, His mercy, which is a free gift.

God is not showing you your sin to condemn you but to condemn the sin and save you (Rom. 8:1-4). Isn't that amazing? What a blessing it is to have this view of God, that any time He's showing me my sin, I know He's not rebuking me. He's rebuking my behavior, but He's actually loving me. It is loving when a parent says to a child, "Stop that! Don't do that!" That's not a law to condemn or destroy; that's a law to help. "I want you to grow up happy, and if you keep doing that, you won't be happy. It's not that I want you to make *me* happy; I want *you* to be happy."

As a lawgiver, Moses cannot show us the Father's true nature. Only Jesus, who was in the Father's bosom, could reveal Him, manifest Him, or show Him (John 1:17-18). Jesus introduced the Father as "Abba," which means Daddy (Mark 14:36; Rom. 8:15). He revealed that the only thing the Father requires of us is not obedience, but just to believe (Col. 2:6-23; Rom. 3:28; 4:5; John 6:28-29). Faith without works, without love, is not real faith. I'm not talking about that kind of faith. I'm talking about the kind of faith that we have which produces the works, but I wasn't the one who produced them (Gal. 2:20; James 1:25). I didn't do them. I just agreed to it because His love was so overwhelming that I kept looking at Him loving me, and I didn't even notice that I was loving others (2 Cor. 3:17-18). I wasn't paying attention to that. And I wasn't taking credit for it because I wasn't even aware of it. If I were, I probably would've tried to take a little credit. I'd just have to ask forgiveness again. But I keep looking at Jesus loving me, not at me loving Jesus. I'm not looking at how I'm loving; I'm looking at how He's loving me. That's what changes me (2 Cor. 3:17-18).

If holiness is used to make us obey, it's a false religion (Rom. 9:30-32). But if it's used to make us believe, it's a true religion (Rom. 3:19-28; 5:20-21; Gal. 3:22-24). The idea of forgiveness started, not with Jesus, but with the Father: "The Father Himself loveth you" (John 16:27). Is God a loving Father or an angry Judge? "The Father Himself loveth you." Indeed, that's why He is holy because He's merciful. God is holy (face one) because He is merciful (face two). His holiness drives me to His mercy, which is then completed by His power. His holiness is not that He is holy in Himself, but rather His holiness is that He is holy in Himself on your behalf: for you, in you, and through you. Holiness is mercy! That is to say, mercy proceeds out of holiness. Otherwise, God wouldn't be holy. If it doesn't lead to mercy, it's not holy. God's holiness cannot be divorced from His mercy (Exod. 15:13; 25:22; 26:34). Therefore, holiness actually is love (Heb. 4:16). It is love that showed you holiness first, even though it's an alien picture of God. He showed you His holiness first so you wouldn't do anything so that you would know only He could do it (Rom. 7:18-24; Gal. 2:19). Then He could give you a free gift through His mercy (Rom. 4:5). And then He gives you the power of the Holy Spirit to prove it (Eph. 1:13; Phil. 4:13). That's beautiful! Do you see? There's more gospel than there is law. The law is one thing, but the gospel is two things. The gospel is mercy plus power (Titus 3:5). The law came through Moses, but mercy, grace, and power came through Jesus Christ. Jesus just keeps going on and on! Because relationship is better than a performance (Heb. 8:7-13).

Under performance, what do you get? Let's say you did everything right and were perfect like Jesus; what would you get? Nothing. Because the law is just the law; that's just what you're supposed to do. You don't get any credit for it. You don't get any reward for it (Luke 18:9-14; Rom. 4:4; Gal. 3:12). What did you do extra? You didn't do anything extra. How could you be better than God? But no one has ever even done that! It's silly even to ask, "What if I were perfect?" Well, you're not. Okay, but what if you were? It would still be nothing because you're just a servant under the law. That's what people do when they're paid. They just do what they have to do, and once you're paid, that's it (Luke 17:9). There's no relationship. God never wanted that. He never wanted to pay anybody (Rom. 11:35-36). He doesn't want to pay anybody. He wants a relationship. He's not looking for servants. He's looking for sons (Gal. 4:3-11). God is a loving Father. He's not an angry Judge. This is very good teaching. It is very strong. You'll have to chew on it a hundred thousand times until you get it.

Most churches do not emphasize the fact that God is our loving Father. They would rather depict God as an angry Judge, emphasizing man's obedience and performance. When we picture God as an angry Judge, we become afraid that He will condemn us for our sins and our guilt. The Bible says, however, that there is now no condemnation for them that are in Christ Jesus (Rom. 8:1). Our religion is relationship-based, not performance-based (John 14:20; Gal. 2:20). When we know that God is our loving Father, we will understand that the only thing He requires of us is faith in His loving promises (Heb. 8:6). It isn't obedience to His commands, it's faith in His promises. That's what He wants as a loving Father. If we are taught that God is an angry Judge, as most people are, then we will believe He demands obedience from us. Jesus said, "This is the work of God, that you believe" (John 6:29). I would think He would say, "This is the work of God, that ye obey." Did you notice the difference? If I'm under the law, that's what it would be. But He wants to show His face and does so through Jesus. "This is the work of God," and the Jews said, "Yeah, that's good, keep the law of Moses." No! He says, "This is the work of God: that you believe." Well, that's not the same thing. If I believe, that's right-hand. If I obey, that's the left hand. Don't let the left hand know what the right hand is doing. Don't do that. Go to the right hand!

Get on God's right hand! Why? That's mercy, and it starts with mercy. I know I'd rather start with mercy. If I start on the left hand of God, I will run into trouble (Rom. 9:31-33; Heb. 3:17-19). I better run over to His right hand and get a different foundation, a better picture of God. Maybe God isn't an angry Judge; maybe He's a loving Father. Let's find out. Unless God had shown it to me, I wouldn't have known. I would only know that

He is an angry Judge. I would never know that He's a loving Father. That's why Jesus came to say, "Look, I'll prove it to you. I will not give you a law. I will give you a gospel, and you'll kill me." Do you know why men killed Him? They killed Him because they didn't want to be loved (John 3:16-20).

People don't mind the law; they'll thank you for that. They hate it when you love them. Do you know why? Because they hate themselves (2 Tim. 2:25-26). They hate themselves because they're sinful and wicked and don't know God. Therefore, when you love a person who hates themselves, you will get hurt. If you love a person, don't think they'll thank you. "Oh, that person is so unloving. You know what, I'm going to love them, and then they'll appreciate it." They'll kill you instead. They will hate you for it because they think, "How stupid of you to love me. I'm no good. I don't even love myself. Stop loving me." They will kill you and do everything they can to make you run away rather than stay there and get killed. "I'm trying to help you!" "Get away from me! I'm poison. I'm bad. I don't want you to love me." People do not want to be loved. And when Jesus came to love the Jewish people, they killed Him (John 1:4-5). Isn't that amazing? It's the same thing in relationships. Human relationships are exactly the same. If someone feels unloved – and that's everyone – they don't want to be loved. Until you kill Jesus, you won't know what love is. You have to kill Jesus yourself. You have to realize, "You know what? I did not like Jesus. And I didn't like God the Father either. When He sent His Son, I just killed Him." But that's exactly what He wanted. He hoped you would do that; He wanted you to do it. Don't you think He could've not drunk the cup? Don't you think He could've said to the Father, "Father, I don't want to drink this cup?" But He said, "I want to drink that cup. I came to drink that cup. I came to be killed (John 12:27-28). I want them to kill me so that when I'm done, I will say on the Cross, "Father, forgive them, for they don't know what they're doing" (Luke 23:34). That's what the law does (1 Cor. 15:56; Rom. 7:21-24). It makes us murderers because it's telling us, "Be good, or I'll kill you!" But you'll say, "I don't want to be good. It's making me mad. I'm under pressure, so I'll just kill Jesus instead." And when it was done, He said, "Father, forgive them." He wasn't angry at all. He was happy. He loved those people. He loved the Jewish leaders. He loved them. He hated what they were doing, but He loved them. He was reaching out to them. When you love someone, when you're in a relationship with someone, if you really have a good relationship, there will be hatred there. This proves that love was seen, and love will be killed. I don't want you to love me because then I'd have to kill you. I'd have to kill you because I'm no good. I'm no good until I meet Jesus and realize that, after I kill Him, He just jumps up again and says, "Okay, I still love you." "What?! After what I just did? You better get away from me." "You can't kill me now." Do you see that? I knew when my wife was free in the marriage because she could come out and do a little bit of sin. I knew she was starting to break down a little. But when she could do a lot of sin, I knew she was really beginning to understand. And when she could really come out, in her fiercest, most angry, and bitter way, then I knew, "Now she loves me." The point is, you don't accept love until you're wicked. You can't even know what love is until you're utterly wicked, you apart from Christ, and you're finally letting out your unregenerate self. She would say to me, "Yes, you love me because you're a Christian and you have to." "Yes, that's true, I am a Christian, but I don't have to. I want to. I'm not going anywhere. I love you." "Well, you're only saying that because you don't really know me." But I think I do. Because if I don't love her, I just said I did, but I really don't, I'll run away. But if I truly love her, she can be anything she wants to be, and I'll still love her. We will only hurt the people that love us because what we're really saying is, "Do you really love me?" "Yes, I do, with the love of God that is working in me and working through me." And they'll say, "Then what about this?" If you can survive that, you've got a relationship. You want to marry someone who sees you as you are, utterly debauched and depraved. And if they can love you that way, you've got a relationship, not a performance. Most marriages are just a performance. Most church worship is just performance (Mark 2:17; 1 Tim. 1:15).

God does not demand or expect human obedience or performance from us (Phil. 1:6; 1 Thess. 5:23-24). Instead, He has given us two gifts to show us His great love and truth: the first is mercy, and the second is power (Titus 3:4-6). He does not want a performance. He does not want legalism (Heb. 13:20-21). He doesn't want us to pretend on the outside. He's a loving Father. If you know His heart, you'll take His mercy and His power. God is our loving Father and shows us His mercy by sending His Son, Jesus, as our Savior, by shedding His Blood for us on Calvary. "God commended His love toward us that, while we were yet sinners, Christ died for us" (Rom. 5:8). He loves us. And that's what a father does – he shows mercy to his children (Luke 15:11-24).

Because God is our loving Father, He not only shows us mercy but also His power by sending us His Holy Spirit as our Sanctifier. The Blood justifies, the Spirit sanctifies (1 Pet. 1:2). He makes us holy by His indwelling presence and the indwelling of the Lord Jesus Christ (John 14:16-17; Eph. 3:16-20). This was the "promise of the Father" spoken of in Jeremiah 31 (Jer. 31:31-34).

God never expects us to obey without His mercy and His power. Whatever God requires of us, He always fulfills Himself. He does it (Gal. 2:20; Col. 1:27; Rom. 8:1-4). If He asks something of you, let Him do it (Phil. 1:6; Eph. 3:20). We can only obey God's will through His mercy and by His indwelling power. He does it all. Whatever He asks of us, He does Himself (1 Thess. 5:23-24).

Although the Father is holy, His justice requires that His holiness must be interpreted through the equity of His mercy (Rom. 3:19-28; Acts 13:39). The letter of the law would kill me so it must be read through the equity of what He originally intended and purposed (Eph. 1:3-14; 3:9-11). God never purposed or intended for you to keep the law (2 Tim. 1:9-10; Rom. 7:4-6). God never wanted you to keep the law (Rom. 5:20). You're not keeping it, and He didn't want you to keep it! He never wants you to keep it. He wants a relationship with you where He can do it through you (Rom. 7:4-6; Gal. 2:19-20). That's why mercy is the first thing He shows you. He shows you the law only so you'll realize you can't keep it; then He gives you the mercy so that you realize you don't have to do a thing (Rom. 5:20; Gal. 3:23-26; 4:3-7). Why? Because in six days, He created the world, and on the seventh day, He rested. He wants you to be at rest. You don't do any work (Heb. 4:1-11). Who created the world? God. What did you do? Nothing. Who redeemed the world? Jesus. What did you do? Nothing. Who's transforming you? The Holy Spirit. What did you do? Nothing. You see, He doesn't want you to do anything! You were not made for work! You were not made for labor! You were not made for power or sweat. You were made for rest (Heb. 4:10-11)! Enter into His rest: the finished work of the Father, the finished work of the Son, and the finishing work of the Holy Spirit, which isn't quite finished because He hasn't transformed you into His likeness and image yet (Rom. 8:29; 2 Cor. 3:18; 1 Thess. 5:23-24). After this lesson, you'll be close. The one thing He wants you to do is nothing (Heb. 4:3-4, 11). That is God's perfect Sabbath Shalom. But you haven't learned to do nothing yet. You still want to do something to prove and establish your righteousness (Gal. 3:1-3).

Although the Father is holy, His justice requires His holiness to be interpreted through the equity of His mercy. Once His holiness is understood in this way, then the power of God affects in our lives what has been declared through the mercy of the Blood of Jesus (Gal. 2:16; Rom. 8:1-4; Titus 3:5).

Love is never forced upon us. We are always free to accept His love or to reject it. If we have the true picture of God, where we see that His holiness is interpreted through His mercy which brings us His power, we will accept His love for us and in us. Let God give you His love through mercy, and then let Him work that in you through the power of the Holy Spirit. He is in you to will and to do. You're not doing anything. Meditate on this one thing: God is a loving Father. He's not an angry Judge. Get the right picture of God and everything else will make sense. If you try to get it with your brain, it won't work. This is not a brain thing. This is a matter of your heart, not your head. Your brain will never accept what I have said. Your brain has to stop because you don't know what perfection is, and you can't get perfection through the law (Heb. 7:19). Perfection comes through the love of Christ, the unconditional love of God (1 John 4:16-19). It is the same in human relationships. You won't have a perfect human relationship until you get rid of the law. No law! It has to be totally mercy.

The grace of the Lord Jesus Christ, and the love of God, and the communion of the Holy Ghost, be with you all (2 Cor. 13:14).

ABOUT THE AUTHOR

James A. Borchert, "Pastor Jim," served continuously in the pastoral ministry for 53 years. He was a well-known pastor and teacher in the Dallas/Fort Worth area and around the world. His library of over 40,000 volumes is a testimony to his dedication to the truth of the Word of God.

Jesus' unexpected revelation of His personal, unconditional love for Pastor Jim, while he was yet a sinner 50 years ago, caused him to love Jesus with all his heart. It was the godly passion behind his ministry.

He held his ordination as a minister of the gospel through World Ministry Fellowship and held numerous teaching seminars and retreats over the years. He taught at Brite Divinity School at Texas Christian University in Fort Worth. He traveled and ministered throughout Sub-Sahara Africa, including the Democratic Republic of Congo, Zimbabwe, Mozambique, Zambia, South Africa, Nigeria, Burundi, and Uganda in an apostolic capacity, training local pastors and teachers since 1984. He also preached and taught in Moldova, India, Ukraine, and Israel. He gave his testimony on The 700 Club and appeared on TBN, sharing the work of Hope for Africa. He and his beloved wife, Peggy, were married for 58 years and had four children and eleven grandchildren before his passing in 2021.

Pastor Jim's insights, through study and prayer, in the areas of theology, discipleship, church government, law, property, trust, and other fields are embraced by both the layman and the scholar.

The heart of Pastor Jim's ministry is discipleship by the revelation of the Holy Spirit and speaking the truth in love so that the church may mature in Him, who is the head, even Christ.

Made in the USA
Columbia, SC
10 February 2024

31244476R00017